HURON COUNTY PUBLIC LIBRARY

P9-CLV-371

77188

917   De Visser, John, 1930-
.132   Southwestern Ontario / photographs by
00222   John de Visser ; introduction by Orlo
DeV   Miller.   Toronto : Oxford University Press,
         c1982.
            90 p. : ill.

         1. Ontario, Southwestern - Description and
         travel - Views.   I. Title.
         019540338X   1520199

Southwestern Ontario

Southwestern Ontario

Photographs by John de Visser *Introduction by Orlo Miller*

Toronto
OXFORD UNIVERSITY PRESS
1982

77188

JUN - 7 1982

© Oxford University Press (Canadian Branch) 1982

ISBN 0-19-540338-K

1 2 3 4—5 4 3 2

Printed in Hong Kong by
EVERBEST PRINTING COMPANY LIMITED

INTRODUCTION
by Orlo Miller

European settlement of Southwestern Ontario was begun in a small way during the early eighteenth century by the French, who cleared farmsteads in several areas along the shore of Lake St Clair and beside the river they called La Tranche, now known as the Thames. But it was not until after the American Revolution that settlement grew to any marked extent, with the arrival of the United Empire Loyalists. Immigrants from Great Britain arrived soon after the Napoleonic Wars, and their numbers reached a peak in the 1840s with a tide of distressed Irish tenant farmers, dispossessed crofters from Scotland, unemployed workers from the new industrial towns of England, and a few prosperous emigrants who were driven to move to Canada by the burdens of taxation at home.

In the first half-century of its modern history, Southwestern Ontario had a rather wild reputation, not unlike that of the later American Southwest. As well as farmers and businessmen, it also attracted adventurers, law-breakers and all sorts of nonconformists. There was an extraordinary mixture of people. One of the noblest chapters of Canadian history was written in the decades before the American Civil War when the towns of Southwestern Ontario offered refuge to more than 25,000 fugitive black slaves who travelled the so-called

underground railroad to freedom in Canada. Though many of the black settlements subsequently disappeared, Dresden and its surrounding area in Kent County still vividly recalls the most famous member of its community, the Reverend Josiah Henson, prototype of the title character in Harriet Beecher Stowe's novel, *Uncle Tom's Cabin*. By contrast, and with grim irony, one of the earliest communities founded by the Society of Friends in 1832 for refugee slaves became nearly fifty years later the site of one of Canada's most notorious murders. At Lucan the grave of members of the Donnelly family is a memorial to forty years of feud and hatred.

The coming of the first railways in the 1850s, the wild land boom and the economic collapse that followed, altered the character of the region forever. For a century afterwards Southwestern Ontario was to be economically, politically, and socially conservative. Fortunes were made, first in land and later in such natural resources as oil, but there was great reluctance to put these fortunes at risk. The patterns of wealth settled into the ownership of large farms and thriving business enterprises in the new towns.

London is the largest city of the region. Situated, not surprisingly, on the Thames River, equidistant between

Toronto and Detroit, it is home to a quarter of a million people. The beautiful University of Western Ontario, the library and art museum, the fine old residences, the cathedral and the parks, are only some of the features that make London a cultural and social focus of Southwestern Ontario. Windsor, the southernmost city in Canada, is one of the nation's most important industrial centres. The third-largest city is Kitchener. Originally founded by Pennsylvania Mennonites at the beginning of the nineteenth century, the settlement was named Berlin by German immigrants a generation later and remained so called until the First World War. The Mennonites of Waterloo County give the city its distinctive character to this day, and many visitors are attracted annually to the colourful farmers' market, famed for its fine produce, excellent cheeses, and Amish delicacies. Sarnia, on the St Clair River, is the petrochemical capital of Eastern Canada. Brantford, on the Grand, has a rich history dating from the arrival of the Mohawks after the American Revolution and including, nearly a century later, an association with Alexander Graham Bell, who conceived the idea of the telephone there. Stratford, on the Avon, attracts nearly half a million people every year to its Shakespearean Festival, which has made the town world-famous.

Today a medley of languages may be heard on the streets of these thriving cities. The campuses of the many universities and community colleges welcome students from every continent. Pin-striped businessmen, with their bulging briefcases, are as busy, and perhaps as harried, as any of their counterparts on Wall Street or at the Bourse. Yet the land remains the same. Not only is it still the most fertile of all Canada's farming areas, but its air is still fresh, its towns and villages friendly, its fields gentle, and its stands of trees luxuriant. Vigorous and varied, yet beautiful and serene, Southwestern Ontario remains one of the most attractive parts of North America in which to live.

1   Dawn south of London

2   Misty morning, Middlesex County

3 Farm near Listowel

4   Eldon House (1834), London

5   Joseph Schneider House (1820), Kitchener

8   Spring blossoms, Kent County

9　St Andrew's United Church, London

10   Restored mill, Elora

11 Roman Catholic Church of Our Lady of the Immaculate Conception, Guelph

13a   Spire of Middlesex College,
University of Western Ontario, London

13b   University College tower,
University of Western Ontario, London

14   Wellington Street, London

15   Storybook Gardens, Springbank Park, London

16   Chatham

17   Middlesex County Courthouse
(1827), London

18   Stockyard market, Waterloo
19   Cattle near Lucknow

20 Ontario Folk Festival, London

21   Labatt's Pioneer Brewery, London

22   Mennonites on their way to church, Waterloo County

23　Mennonite church in Waterloo County, near Kitchener

24   Sparta

25   Farmers' market, Waterloo

26 Garden centre, Essex County
27 Fanshawe Pioneer Village, London

28   Doon Pioneer Village, Kitchener
29   Bell homestead, the home from
1870 to 1874 of Alexander Graham
Bell (1847-1922), near Brantford

30 Bell homestead

31   Memorial at the home of Colonel John McCrae (1872-1918),
author of the poem 'In Flanders Fields', Guelph

32 Festival Theatre from the River
Avon, Stratford
33 Old Town Hall (1851-2), now
the Oxford Museum, Woodstock

34   Courthouse, Stratford, seen across the River Avon

35 Trinity Anglican Church (1836),
Port Burwell

36   Lighthouse at Kincardine

38 The Square, Goderich, built by
William 'Tiger' Dunlop (1792-1848),
who founded Goderich in 1827

39   St Clair River, Sarnia

40　St Paul's, Her Majesty's Chapel
of the Mohawks (1785), Brantford

41   Tombstone of the Donnellys, St Patrick's Cemetery, Lucan

42   John Backhouse's gristmill (1798), Port Rowan, the oldest mill in Ontario

43   'Uncle Tom's Cabin', home of Josiah Henson (1789-1883), Dresden

44   Shakespeare

45   Former Opera House, reflected
in a window, St Mary's

46 CPR station, Goderich
47 Covered bridge (1881), the last
built in Ontario, West Montrose

48 Lake Erie near Port Burwell
49 Old well at Oil Springs, dating from the 1880's, when
Petrolia and surroundings were the oil capital of Canada

50 Steam meet at Ilderton

51 Classic-cars meet at Eagle

52   Ontario fall fair, Listowel

53   Haying, Kamoka

54   Waiting for the school bus, south of London

55 Early morning near London

56 Lake Erie, near New Glasgow
57 Port Dover

58   Ambassador Bridge and the Roman Catholic Church
of the Assumption, from the University Campus, Windsor

59 St Mary's River, near Sarnia

60   Hiram Walker Museum (1811), Windsor

61　Public Library, Sombra

62   Dockyards, Sarnia

63 Winter furrows near Wallaceburg

64   Jack Miner Bird Foundation, a 2000-acre sanctuary,
begun in 1904, near Kingsville

65   Spring barley, near Wingham

66   Early summer near Sparta

67   Lake Erie at the mouth of the Detroit River

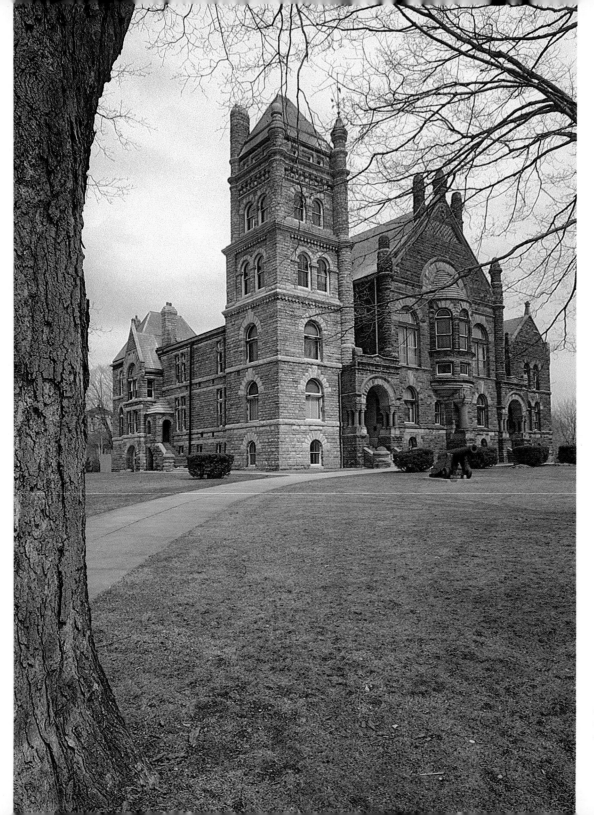

68 Oxford County Courthouse
(1890-2), Woodstock
69 Canadian Legion, Ingersoll

70   Fruit and vegetable market, Seaforth

71 Maple Syrup Festival, Elmira

72   Geese, Waterloo County

73   African Lion Safari and Game Park, Rockton

74 Lake George Park Area, Simcoe
75 River Avon, Stratford

76   Elora Gorge on the Grand River, Elora
77   Waterfall on the Upper Thames River, St Mary's

78   The Thames River at Chatham

79   Point Clark on Lake Huron

80   St Peter's Anglican Church (1827), Tyrconnell
81   Port Stanley

82 Picking beans, Essex County
83 Peppers, Lambton County

84   Fort Malden (1796), Amherstburg

85   Sunflowers, Oxford County

86   Elora
87   Tobacco fields, Elgin County

88   St Clair River, Sarnia

89 Highway 401 near Nilestown, South of London